Writings and drawings herein are the product of Gus M. Woodward II, and he is responsible for the contents. Wider Perspectives Publishing reserves 1st run rights of this work and all rights revert to the author upon delivery. Author then reserves the right to grant or restrict reprinting of this volume in whole or in part and he may resubmit for contests and anthologies at will.

Copyright © Gus M. Woodward II, 2019
December 2019, Norfolk, Va./Wider Perspectives Publishing
1st edition ISBN: 9781712746769
2nd edition July 2020 ISBN: 978-1-952773-16-7

Welcome to <u>Inquire Within, Inspire Within</u>, a collection of Poems by Gus "MC G2" Woodward. This is a look at the forest and the trees, the waves and the seas and even the gentle pushes from the breeze. That is to say that this is a trip through the causes and the effects behind the poet, but if you are open and you let him, he will affect your causes and cause an effect or two – in you.

Come walk with him…

Fuels the Gus   1

Brews Into MC G2   19

Let the Son Receive this Light   35

If She Hears With the Heart   41

Passed Through and Out to All of You   49

Whirls About the Gus   67

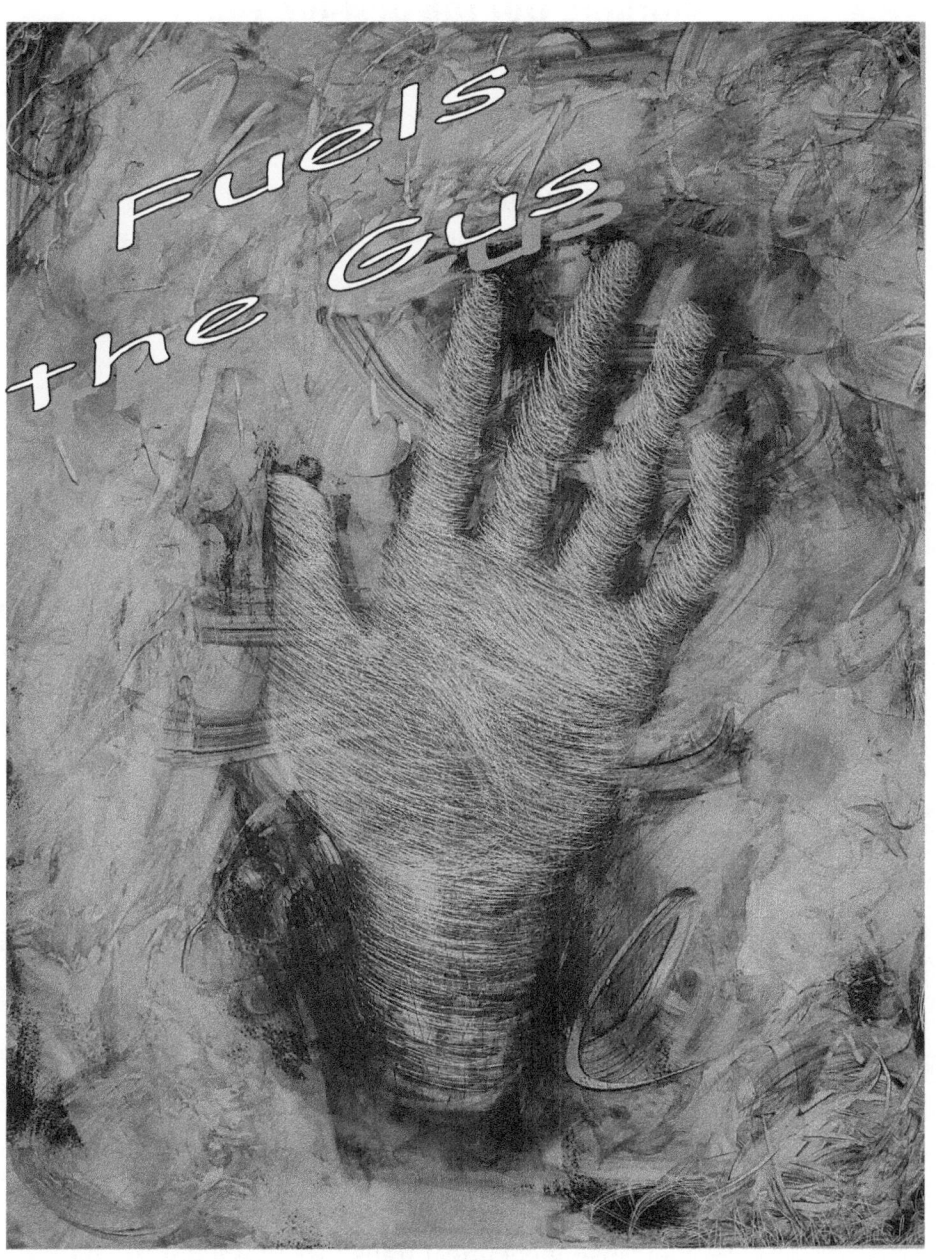

Inspire Within, Inquire Within

<u>Nothing But the Best for You</u>

Wish nothing but the best for you,
Living is all I am dying to do.
Loving is all I am living to do.
Wish nothing but blessings grew,
As you did what you needed to.
Loving is all I am living to do.

Attaining dreams through tackling goals,
no more compartmentalizing roles.
Always reviewing my story and thoughts for holes,
Namasté to diverse and like minded souls!
Spiritual love electricity, sharing unconditionally,
Good for you nutritionally, as we move forward transitionally.
Listen close can you hear the lessons?
See the reflection let out all confessions,
give gratitude for all the blessings.

Wish nothing but the best for you,
Living is all I am dying to do.
Loving is all I am living to do.
Wish nothing but blessings grew,
As you did what you needed to.
Loving is all I am living to do.

Built to make it through,
loving forward is what I do!
Unleashing messages in to the sky,
cleansing chemical trails that fly.
Spitting holy ghost rhymes into the seven seas,

exhaling four winds to please all the suffocating trees,
built to please, built to give and through giving I receive.
Gonna give so much I shine bright even after death,
like light that remains long after the star has left.

Spices

Gave God all of my dice,
using this pen as my knife
to slice and dice.
Got growth cooking into this life,
adding in a whole lot of spice,
coriander & cayenne flavors to entice,
always kind but not always polite,
pacifist but I still remember how to fight.
I know I thrive in the sunlight
but still so addicted to the middle of the night,
that's where my creativity really seems to take flight.
Investing time in harnessing my foresight, insight!
To see deeper than wrong or right,
breaking vibrations down into electrons and protons,
no matter whether you are pros or cons,
we gotta care about more than gold silver and bronze,
no more times of kings rooks and pawns,
growing together as each new day dawns.

Inspire Within, Inquire Within

Unteach Me

Please Lord unteach me all of these fallacies,
cleanse my eyes of all these fake realities.
Finally forming the right mentality,
bringing brothers and sisters vitality,
supplying energy with authentic personality.
Inspiration pouring into my headphones,
loving the under and overtones,
making me think of divine moans,
undeniable the light has grown.
7 wheels flowing smoothly
like an essential oil cologne,
energy up and down my backbone,
spitting ciphers like a cyclone,
same lessons are intricately sewn,
Now more confidently shown
with or without a microphone.

Different, Never Indifferent

May have thought you were ahead of the curve,
couple years pass and already being kicked to the curb.
Addicted to distractions like Snoop is to herb,
addicted to playing with nouns and verb.
No demon shall disturb,
grateful for the angels,
that flew into my life at the right times,
hard times but the light still shines,
my mind can still find patterns and rhymes,

sick of pinching nickel and dimes,
love moments and people, all kinds.
Life's paths intertwine and align
when they're supposed to.
Never how you expect
but ya gotta embrace change,
every person is strange
so God can't be very different,
or rather must be really different,
never indifferent,
through artists voices truth is vociferant.
Please save us from our ignorance.

Consciousness

Consciousness is neurons hallucinating about their existence,
can either let go or hold on to resistance.
World and self playing their roles,
both broken down, into north and south poles,
building a balance of fear and goals.
Hope we find balance,
when we agree on our controlled illusion,
well, that's what we call "reality",
laughter and internal seem to be the key,
to whether hearts agree,
to how the two see.
Let us predict and perceive it all,
hallucinating animals with self-awareness.
We are part of it all, part of all.

Inspire Within, Inquire Within

Sight Set

Dreamcatcher draped over my eyes,
symmetrically shaped with strong ties,
5 feathers dance as time flies.
Sacred patterns and lines,
helping as my mind divines,
truth out of the unclear signs.

Learning to Swim

Pretended I was walking on water
'til I realized I'd been drowning for ages.
Finally got my head above water,
waiting for my potential son or daughter.
When he arrived I knew I had to strive for much more..
than anything I had before.
Now I'm staring at the shore,
spitting songs and folklore.
Stories arise and descend,
relationships end and others mend,
lives begin again every mornin',
set intention as the day is just formin'.
Let some light slip into the gateway,
head towards your fateway.
Balance the work and the play,
let people come and go as they may.

Filling my blood with integrity and respect,
genuine love is all I want to reflect,
messages intention is direct,
spirit coming in full effect.

<u>Learning How to See</u>

As my roots bury themselves deeper into the dirt,
listening to the birds putting on a concert,
seemed to invert my nature of introvert,
even though it provided comfort,
now never scared to assert.
As my branches sway,
leaves whisper, "don't waste today."
Balancing new life and decay in a beautiful array,
admiring the cosmic display
of the night chasing the sunlight in spiraling rhythm,
giving power to the prism, each element is a musician.
Collaborating on a shared composition,
so nice to tune in and listen,
enjoying the loud silences in each transition.
The forest is growing closer to me,
arms open heart free,
I am a universe just learning how to see.

Inspire Within, Inquire Within

Reflection

Sitting alone in the moist sand,
Where the ocean meets the land.
Letting the grains run through my hand.
Rising sun surrounded by ivory,
Felt more intimate than a diary.
Rugged night left me here,
The more light that pours in to these crying eyes
The morning becomes clear.
Ebb and flow of truth and lies.
Sorting through the voices and choices.
Letting the tide take the broken memories.
This new day has no space for regrets.
Thank you sky for your kindness,
Curing me of my blindness.
Thank you pain for reminding me I feel,
Never again will you have my trust
Never again will there be an us.
Thank you pain for reminding me
I feel.
Thank you ocean song for singing
This melodic melody.
As the tide now rises inside,
Throwing a message in a bottle
Along with my misused pride.
The wind carries cares off my shoulders.
Truly appreciate every step of growing older.
Thank you pain for reminding me I feel
Thank you love for making life real.

Still Standing

Hummingbirds and truffula trees,
swaying beautifully in the breeze.
Reminds me of love songs that always please,
And at the same time how everyone leaves.
At least that's the way it seems,
until we tear apart the seams.
Taking down the walls,
letting go like waterfalls.
Happy to run anytime my external heart calls,
happy to brave the strongest squalls.
Striving to sit in the stillness behind the mind,
the most peaceful place inside
I've ever been able to find.
Helping me to unwind,
without having to push rewind.
Determined to find
all the ways I have been and am blind,
to my world and what I've been missing.
Used to think it was all about who I was kissing,
Now I care about the ones that are really listening.
To the truth my spirits always whispering.
Excited to see where friends stories will lead,
I believe my love always plants a seed.
Wanna be open and easy to read,
like a book so worn
the spine is almost torn,
but still standing with more
inside than on the cover.

Inspire Within, Inquire Within

Always there but never trying to hover,
every day there's something new to discover,
through the pain I recover,
a way to help every other,
father friend sister son and mother.
I am a freedom fighter and a lover,
still standing with so much more
inside than on the cover.

Rainy Morning

Rain making the pavement wet,
opportunity in the air mindset,
truth's I never want to for-get.
On people I never expect
but I'll put down the biggest bet,
especially if we let.
Each other in- as a real friend,
trust is a holy attribute, letting Appreciation's rays shoot,
never trying to dispute,
someone else's story or thoughts.
unforgivable shots, that make all kinds of relationships rot,
at the core, cannot ignore another's feelings.
respect the secrets they're concealing,
we can all help each other with healing
but only if we're willing, constantly instilling, distilling.
Emptying reviewing and refilling.

Fairgrounds Cafe

Conversations with a stranger,
no room for any fear or anger...
Esoteric ideas and perspectives,
turning dreams into directives.
Imaginations eclectic, kindness is my elective,
never been overly selective.
I love humanity,
even through all the darkness and vanity,
even through my own insanity.
I find common threads,
like walking through God's dreads,
never locked, even when reality gets rocked,
I move with it, getting smooth with it,
just trying to find every groove,
never win or lose,
more like new connections I fuse.
Sorting through feeling that used to confuse,
used to keep me in the blues,
now I love seeing from other shades and shoes.
Empathy experience imbues the clues to the internal news,
I need to proceed, spirit needs to feed to take the lead,
stop fueling the fire of selfish desire,
stop giving power to the liar.
A simple stop at the coffee shop
and now I feel on top
of the moment, trying to share not trying to own it.
I don't want to rest I have to hone it.

Inspire Within, Inquire Within

Gifted by these observations,
paintings, and decorations,
life should be a celebration.
Willing to give my whole participation,
to the illumination of our present elevation.

Free Will

If it was all preordained
we wouldn't know how to build our own lane,
wouldn't be as fun without mistakes while we maintain.
Wouldn't have joy of the sun without some good rain.
Without all this pain life wouldn't be the same,
hollow existence, with no need for resistance,
no need to work, no need for persistence...
We just need to change the consistency,
exchange entitlement for accountability,
along with love it is a heavenly ability.
Exchange our internal duality for unity,
with all the changes I see seems soon to me,
that we can conquer our self-defeat.
No need for retreat,
life's struggle is spirit reminding ourselves we are complete,
remind ourselves of the parts that taste so sweet,
to savor each memory.
Remind us we need to dig deeper for our legacy
so our family is proud of our history.
So let's carve our own manifest destiny,
thank you, creator, for blessing me,
for transforming me from diamond out of coal

from the pressure and stress in me.
I know I can't give up
'cause you still left this breath in my chest
and set my soul free, let my true eye see,
how if I want to make it
in this heavy current I just have to be.
Have to believe in more than me,
but believe in me,
that I can help create this better reality
with no more duality.
The proof is how easily,
authentic connection inspires me.

Sacred Geometry (Geo-me-TREE)

Multicolored tree running
through all seven seas.
Although the body grows frail,
the shine will align no fail,
Kundalini perfectly intertwined
balanced female and male,
flower of life bursting from the crown,
halo aura shining all around.
Just resting in lotus, sharpening focus
listening for the words creator wrote us,
passing through the tree of life channel,
receiving as much wisdom as anyone can handle,
each chakra warmly lit like a candle.
Hands uplifted for this breath we're gifted,
each perfect direction life has shifted,

Inspire Within, Inquire Within

no longer saddened when relationships drifted,
the plot was always meant to be twisted,
remaining optimistic and creatively prolific.
Personal providence is made of elements
of perception and intelligence,
won't hurt to give loved ones compliments,
and affirming love statements.
Unconditionally is the only way to truly display,
when heart shines brighter than a sun ray,
let us bring color to a world gone gray.

Express

Letting these festering feelings feast,
silence can be a bitter beast.
I am writing it out at least,
letting the pen focus all these emotions,
blank pages welcome the new ink oceans.
Please accept this confession,
let this be another lesson,
I earn from,
not just burn from,
but learn from.
Feels like a sharp ton,
stopping my tongue
until the moments over and done.
I was supposed to have fun,
but here I am with none.

Why is it I care less about what most call a good time?
Do my absolute best just to not spit out a rude line
because always supposed to be so kind.
Lemme just borrow the purple crayon,
so I can write all over these walls,
bringing myself back down,
until all this weight falls.
Rising again to meet the next moment.

<u>Energy Plus Motion</u>

E plus motion equals emotion,
Energy that we put into motion,
an all encompassing ocean.
Understanding and awareness are the potion,
to navigate through confusion and commotion.
Constant need to clarify,
especially when tensions are high,
to find out where loyalties lie.
No one wants to be the bad guy,
so might as well say sorry and try,
to mend relationships
before they become sunken ships.
Ego please allow spirit to eclipse,
everyone could use some forgiveness,
use those lips to make stress loose it's grips,
on those people living like it's the apocalypse.

Inspire Within, Inquire Within

Give light until it slips, into their core,
until they're hungry for more, share as we explore,
and remember to never ignore,
that best friend within!
In fact if you have forgotten again,
that is exactly where we need to begin.

Family Compilation

I blame my family for infecting me
with inspiration of all kinds,
I am the mix CD compilation of their 4 minds.
Thanks Dad
for showing me that happiness is my choice,
thanks Mom
for helping me find my artistic voice.
Michael
appreciate all the times you took me under wing,
whole self is what you always bring,
Jennifer thank you
for the encouragement and amazing music,
first time playing guitar was your acoustic.
Mixed with some influences from the outside,
when they saw me struggling to survive
they helped me to guide my glide.
Need balance along this roller coaster ride.
Help helps when it's your turn to drive,
I want to help each of you thrive,
uplift each of our little tribes,
sharing love trust and good vibes.

Thank you God for such an amazing family,
protecting our sanity through sickness and calamity.
Thank you now for this son of my own,
crazy how fast all of our kids have grown,
Gage, Riley, Bodhi and Cadence!
Perseverance and patience,
rising from this jungle,
you will surely stumble,
just accept the challenge and remain humble,
and remember we always got your back,
when it feels like you're under attack.
So grateful to my family for filling me with inspiration of all kinds,
I am the collaborative painting of their 4 hearts and minds.

Inspire Within, Inquire Within

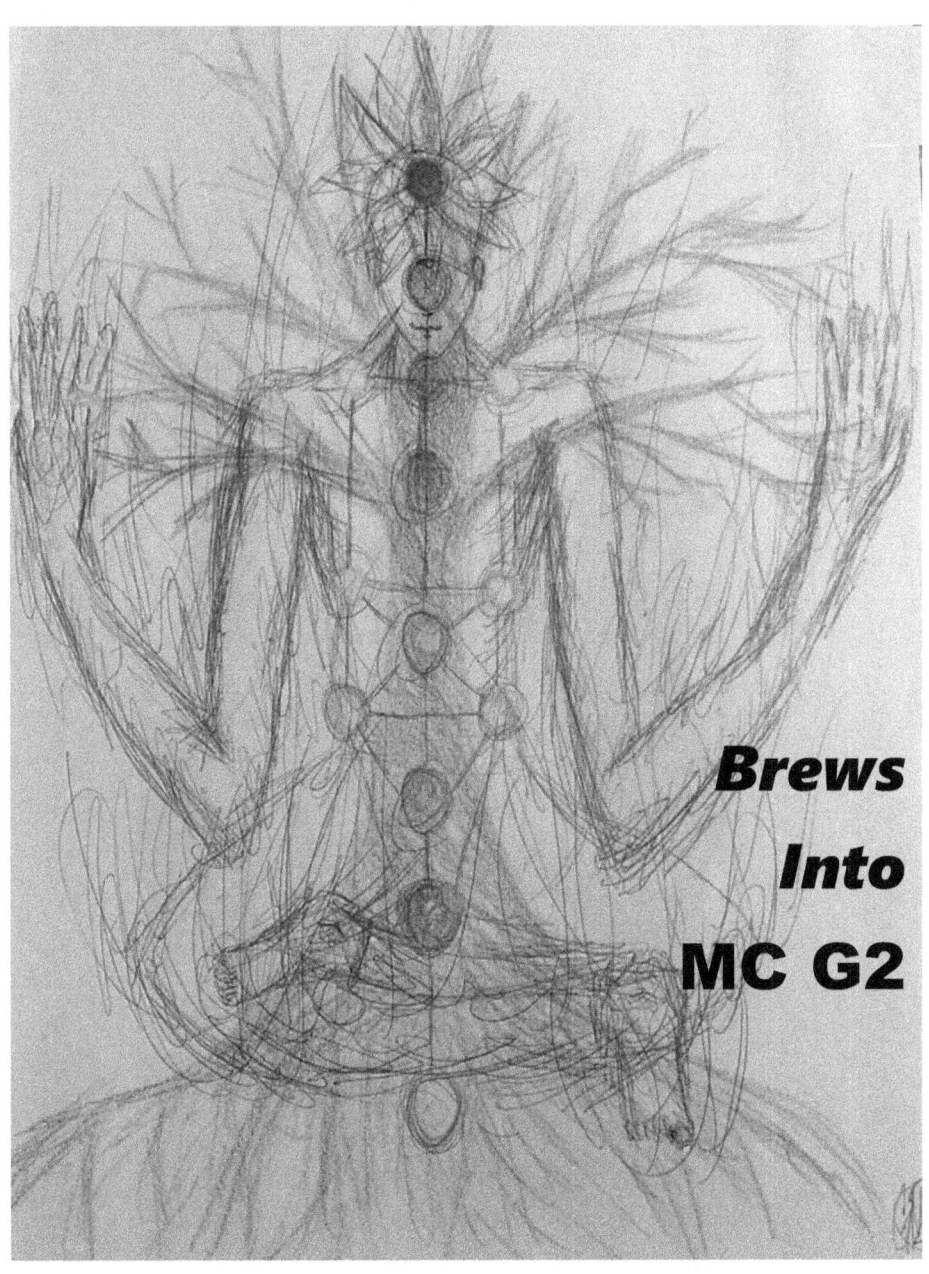

Inspire Within, Inquire Within

Growth

The voices inflection,
gives words life and direction.
Never meant to just lie on the paper,
dying to fly off like air vapor,
born with a message and a meaning.
Used to be unbalanced in my dreaming,
til I began to do some internal cleaning.
Thoughts became clearer,
no longer clouded with fear,
loving the man in the mirror,
come so far from wishing I could disappear.
Always wanted to fly away,
ride Windstreams into a different day.
When my super son arrived,
I began to truly dive,
harder and smarter I continue to strive
to always provide a way to do more than survive,
teach him we are here to help everyone thrive!

Mountain of Metaphor

Closer we get to the mountain top,
the more we want to stop, drop,
and roll like the ice and snow,
when the warmth begins to grow.
Right now it's as if time has begun to slow,
almost like waiting for ourselves to grow,
longer we wait to live the longer we have to go,

so might as well let go of every comfort zone.
Reminder! these bodies are only on loan,
our souls probably aren't even ours to own,
they belong to the collective,
to which we all add perspective.
I continue to climb,
with each well placed rhyme,
I get a little closer,
wrapping up all you need like your local grocer.
Transformed the mountain into music and I am the composer.

Piano Player

Fingers delicately dance,
piano putting listeners into a trance.
The player takes a quick glance,
whole room is now on their feet,
couldn't stay in the seat
with a melody so sweet...
Chance for destined lovers to meet,
then enters a pulsating back beat.
Making the rhythm even more complete.
Both hands become a blur,
as the folks on the floor really begin to stir.
Synchronicity starts to occur,
the forgotten remembering who they were,
good vibes in the air like frankincense and myrrh.
Music is a magic whisperer,
but only if your soul allows the healing to enter.

Inspire Within, Inquire Within

Writing as Therapy

I needed the lines more than they needed me to write them,
seeds of emotions take root and start to stem,
letting the worlds flow I shine brighter than a gem,
spitting out better things than an ATM,
sharing the essence,
of omnipresence until my souls evanescence.
I found my element,
a way to make these abstract thoughts relevant,
not scared to point out the elephant,
story teller so gonna add some embellishment
but I know the truth is delicate like a skeleton
and I would not compromise that precious medicine.

Wished I Was

Growing up always wanted to be wolverine,
not for admantium claws so pristine,
more for the healing power,
and strength to never cower.
Wanted to be Spider Man,
soaring higher than any bird can,
shooting webs to wrap up evil.
helping and saving people,
always rising up after a fall,
sharing internal lessons with the fourth wall,

as I continue to answer the call.
Of being a hero and balancing it all.
Not to mention that amazing spider sense,
hyper aware of the present tense.

Inquire Within, Inspire Within

Inquire within, inspire within
the best parts will blend.
All of me is what I send,
from beginning to end.
Brokenhearted world
but it's ours to mend.
No need to defend,
assumption is a judgment
and always offends.
Somehow it's worked itself
into our daily trends.
Carrying fear and hate
just makes the spine bend.
We've gotta stop dreaming
our lives away.
And live the dream
'cause it's all play anyway.
Nothing's what it would seem.
Just have to love life and live it!
Earn trust and give!
Love life and live it!
Earn trust then freely give it,
to all who hear.

Inspire Within, Inquire Within

Help them see clearer,
remember everyone
has their own kind of fear.
Just get their back
and give encouraging cheer.
Eye to eye a man to his peers
Another breakthrough
Is already here.

Pen Strokes

Just a few lines in the right place, start to form a face,
few more and we can start to picture a time and place,
turn it around just as quickly and erase,
or at the very least repair or replace,
more lines shading details,
imagining now if our hero wins or fails?
What were the stakes and the scale?
What type of enemy was trying to derail?
More lines give life to the tale.
Is this character's portrait solo,
or is there a team or family as the picture continues to grow?
Some come and some go,
some real ones have stayed though.
Carefully drawn representations,
of my greatest affiliations,
with divine incarnations,

I can hear all of your soul mix compilations.
Just a few lines and I try to convey symbols and signs,
of a world that shines.
Appreciation for the pain and good times,
intertwined with magic miracles of all kinds.

Finish Line

Finish line but I'm never stopping,
past self I have to keep topping,
passion is never dropping!
30 for 30 and the days flew,
practicing this verbal jujitsu,
to my word I stayed true,
and this month of work is just a preview.
These april showers, bringing May flowers,
awakened more of my poetic powers.
This challenge truly helped me on some days,
tested me in other ways, Love the way my mind plays,
with words that are filtered through my spirit.
Opportunity seldom knocks, so when it does don't fear it.

Leveling Up Awareness

Not really trying to be this contradiction,
more than the sum of my addiction.
Made up of a whole lot of truth and fiction,

Inspire Within, Inquire Within

just catching some friction,
working on my next verbal depiction.
Negativity captured by my diction,
Transformed into personal refreshment,
pouring in an investment of reflection,
never scared to ask the hard question,
screw life of ignorant guessing,
more awareness is my main obsession.

Shape the Spiral

Minds writing rhymes all the time,
calling out glaring crime,
the ones we all see and any of mine,
not trying to stiffen my spine
I'm here to align.
Like earth sun and moonshine.
Determined to do more than climb,
Building bridges like Gustave Eiffel,
will not allow anything to stifle,
sharp aim faster than a rifle,
guardian like my brother Michael.
Gonna learn and shape the spiral,
not repeat the same cycle,
chill but never idle,
fight for more than survival,
renaissance revival.

Honing Vision

Licking my wounds,
tomorrow always comes too soon,
just trying to relax and watch life bloom,
yet always feels like I got too much to do,
enjoyed a second and time flew.
Trying to memorize all the lessons as I grew,
mastery is my target,
willing to work the hardest,
practice til I can go the farthest,
with precision
allowing God in for every decision.
Honing my vision,
forethought and foresight
without forgetting not to get too uptight,
surrounded by light,
surrounded by loved ones,
trading love in gallons and tons.
Your matter matters,
see the benefit in the chutes and ladders.
Take two steps back
but review the knowledge
you may have lacked,
don't let your feelings help you slack.

Inspire Within, Inquire Within

Phoenix Burning

Flames rose with a whole new ferocity,
spirit rising with a whole new philosophy,
always loved reciprocity while maintaining autonomy,
using everything my parents taught me,
make motivation and joy intrinsic,
try to view the world as if everything is artistic.
And we are the artists and architects,
up to us to redirect this shipwreck
and reconnect with the present
and remind ourselves life is already perfect,
it's just never gonna be what you expect.

Moment of Silence

Sitting in this elaborate temple,
just a man so very simple.
Letting negatives develop this film role,
learning the purpose of my life's role.
Simple soul complicated by my mind at times
when I'm a little less aligned.
Never scared to grind,
just don't allow the sparks to blind,
as you find so shall you unwind.
Freedom isn't free!
Takes a lot of time and passion to be,
takes focus to see.

Throwing prayers in the air,
sending love everywhere,
don't be scared of the nightmare,
it's an illusion to tear through
to find out more about you.
Me I'm just a man very simple
but got a universe hiding in this temple,
balancing physical spiritual & mental.

How Do I Feel?

How do I feel? Depressed and stressed
if I don't remind myself every second I'm blessed
to have breath in these upside down trees in my chest.
Never have need to conceal,
hurts being less than real.
How do I feel? Here's the deal,
Tired but got no time for rest,
not with all this zest
to give the world better than my best.
Got to master this craft,
desperate rhymes like it's my life's raft,
not wasting a second of past,
going to make these scribbles last,
using music to carry it fast.
How do I feel? Feel like I have a to-do list into infinity,
the type that doesn't deflate but is ever filling me,
set fire to this will in me.

Inspire Within, Inquire Within

Deep End, Deepened, Depend

Hoodie with my Horus eye hanging from my neck,
got 4th-dimensional warriors on deck,
projecting this proverbial blank check.
Spirit guide that can no longer hide,
no longer disguise the Technicolor tie dye
lights pouring from my eyes.
Tongue delivering cleansing flames, got no time for lies and games.
Going against the grain, but more natural than rain,
used to be so scared of losing, now all I do is gain.
Two hands with all kinds of purpose,
metamorphosis will convert this, vessel-- inside and surface.
Living in the deep end,
my love for life has deepened,
unconditional it doesn't depend,
only way to transcend is to let paints blend,
in a fashion that will make minds bend,
hearts and soul's mend with the families they live within.
Community through patience, no treating people like patients.
Humanity through kindness, ignorance is what blinds this,
there's a way through and we can find Bliss.
Heighten our awareness,
expand our consciousness.
Up to us to further this.

Shadow Boxin'

Shadow boxin' with every toxin,
no more time for simply talking,
so much conviction it's shocking.
Climbing the waterfall of emotion,
before they get me lost in the ocean.
prayed for a raft, the messenger laughed,
told me, "You asked for this path,
so keep swimming, keep walking, keep crawling,
breathe deep when it feels like you're falling.
It'll be hard to live the calling,
at least you get to choose the weight you're hauling."
I close both Fists, Knuckles made of moldavite and amethyst,
protecting this slice of Bliss,
adjusting my eyes to see through the mist.
Invisible villains, never seem to stop spilling,
I am a prophecy fulfilling, quantum warrior Lord willing,
void filling, fear killing. Sacrifice unseen, like a lost dream.

Hope vs Faith

Hope avoids the fire while faith walks through!
Hope is Band-Aids and faith is gorilla glue!
Hope is a beggar asking for donations,
Faith is the foundation of the strongest creations.
Faith is a rocket ship that leaves hope behind.
Hope is still just wishing on a star to find,
Something that will make him brave like faith
Not scared of inner and outer space.

Inspire Within, Inquire Within

There is no substitute for true faith,
Teamed with true love no force could replace.
An energy so powerful and humble,
Like making a dance out of a stumble.
Seeing the beauty in life's jungle,
Under pressure hope tends to crumble,
Faith always prepares you to rumble.
Faith is a melodic shout, hope just a mumble.
Which ones for you? know which one I choose!
Inking affirmations that sink like tattoos.
I refuse to misuse or make any excuse,
I refuse to balance halfway hope and the blues.
I am here to infuse from crown to shoes,
Faith and love are an almighty muse,
Along with all of you on this cruise,
Along with all of the beautiful views.
Moments and memories we never lose.
Raised my false hopes from the grave,
Resurrected into a Phoenix of faith.

Nature is Listening

I told the clouds to move
so I could see the moon.
It was dope 'cause they did almost as soon,
as my thought became spoken,
old barriers became broken,
new powers have awoken.

Inner Child

I'm just a little boy that's dying to play,
but my adult side keeps me in all day.
Saying it's not realistic to live that way,
then the inner child starts to say...
"If you let me out, you also let go of doubt,
doesn't that sound like the right route?"
The adult starts to shout,
"I got money to make and bills to pay!"
"We also have a soul
that isn't fake and have to let it play."
How can we merge these sides?
Making it one instead of two separate rides,
put new transparencies on top of life's slides,
be the director of what's on your overhead projector.
Don't be a follower be a curious inspector.
If we have the power to pretend
let's put an end to attempting to defend,
you gotta be your hearts best friend,
that way when you lend, a hand or an ear,
it's to actually help or hear
from a place that's sincere,
not just fake listen
while your eyes glisten.
Join the story your missing,
don't let someone else write your mission,
don't lose yourself to wishing,
pretending is just a means to use imagination for new creation,
all starts with a thought,
all starts with being aware of the way we are taught,
acknowledge the traits that still need to be fought.

Inspire Within, Inquire Within

Injustices and ignorance cannot be found
unless you're willing to break new ground.
Get away from the known,
only person that can ever really hone
you is your own inner child,
so let 'em light a fire that runs wild.

MC G2

Inspire Within, Inquire Within
Shine Harder Through the Darkness

I will not allow this little cloud,
to stop me from shining,
even more important through hard timing.
Will not let him slip from my mind,
dedicating every bit of my shine,
manifesting every kind,
sending love from every part,
of my patched together heart.
From the air in each lung,
to the poems bouncing off my tongue,
all the songs I'll sing and have sung,
are filled with every single bit,
of light and love that a father can fit,
with my whole spirit I commit to never quit!

Healing!

Powerless is having a child that is ill,
want to wage war against the ailment with your full will,
but they need you to be tender and sit still.
There is no perfect pill it's just about trying instill,
feelings of love and safety,
keeping it together when you know it's making you crazy.
Just want to heal my baby,
this happens too often lately.

MC G2

Words of healing I speak,
words of healing please go and seek,
every thing making my son's body feel weak,
using any and every spiritual technique.
Spirit guides and angels here this plea,
help me heal with energy like Edgar Cayce!

S.I.N.

I made it further today, not saying I didn't make mistakes along the way. I am trying to say I made it further today, in what way? Well since awareness is key, not just key to how to treat you, more importantly key to how to treat me. Because if I have nothing good within, I have nothing for family or friend, if I have nothing within, I have nothing to send, no way to ascend, all I have is s.i.n. get up again, only way is to take the trash in the bin, replace it with the true you like recyclin'. All the s.i.n.-- self inflicted negativity, is what triggers sensitivity, depression and anxiety, angry and entitled society, but can't change that unless I know how to change what's inside of me, all the I am power, shining the light from the top of the tower, learning to enjoy both sweet and sour, because each moment only lasts for so long, waiting on being right for so long it all goes wrong. Find your meaning and turn it in to a song, I made it a little further today, not looking the other way, saying yes son I always want to play. I made it a little further today, and tomorrow I am going to keep pushing forward and thank the source for every second! Past future and most of all present!

Inspire Within, Inquire Within

Guilt

Hard not to feel the guilt,
side effects from the new life I've built.
Sacrificing the most precious time,
suffering from my own crime,
to earn more nickels and dimes.
At it's best it's a moral compass to guide,
other times it's eating you from the inside.
Miss my son but I know I need to provide,
and I am qualified for the job in which I applied,
overwhelmed when first jumping on the ride
but now I found my stride.
Still impossible to hide,
from the guilt that cannot be denied,
feeling like I'm just off to the side,
watching my son grow
becoming more like a TV show.
Sometimes makes me feel like vertigo,
trading quality time for opportunity and more dough,
to combat the guilt I continue to work on myself though,
with words I paint like Van Gogh,
therapeutic inspirational tornado,
but not gonna miss today in exchange for tomorrow,
cannot live in shame and sorrow.
After I let this role borrow,
some of my time as I master the rhyme,
communication and leadership skills becoming sublime!
All the while my love will forever shine,
Bo will always know he's on my mind.

MC G2

His heart is always in mine
and he's the fire in my spirit,
gonna make sure the whole world can hear it.
Not for appearance, watch this perseverance!!
Pushing even after my physical disappearance.

Inspire Within, Inquire Within

If She Hears With the Heart...

Inspire Within, Inquire Within

Sunday

Wake up in the morning ready to sacrifice, end of the day never regretting the price, if I am not sure about a mistake I make it more than twice, getting ready and addressing each vice, that which does not belong I slice, listening to the mirrors better advice, life is an artist's paradise. Not racing with the rats nor mice, cheese in the trap doesn't even entice. We see the canvas in every campus, beautiful canvas helps us innerstand this. Get to know your personal idea OF bliss, before it's too late and you miss, every chance too focused on the abyss, while angels fighting to give you their kiss. Feel the power I can clearly see, believe in yourself even half as much as me. Got excess belief to provide relief to those blinded by their grief. Sitting on an imaginary reef, hiding their smile underneath. I see you shining like a new day, communicating the best way, through action and the right words to say, trying to do work with the same passion that children play. Hey it's nice to truly just see you each Sunday.

Magic

Impossible for a poet not to notice
First time she caught my focus.
Her eyes were in a trance,
like her soul was in this intense dance.
She concealed galaxies within her curls,
Constellations and other worlds,
anytime her expression unfurls,
it's full of diamonds and pearls.
She takes deep breaths of wisdom,
absorbs all 7 from the prism.

On a whole new system
thanks to her intuitive vision.
Executing with a high level of precision.
Some may not see
But that's probably
Just depending on the frequency.
It's more than clear to me,
her fairy dust is affecting
everyone she connects with,
Helping others open their gift.
She is the spiritual locksmith.
Just go ahead and let her uplift.

Head and Heart Space

Have to reveal how you feel, tell the sweet girl what is real. Because she deserves to know, deserves to get up and go. You know without you she will grow, her light will continue to glow, and isn't that the hope as the river continues to flow. The people on the path that you pass may last or may pass by fast, we don't get to choose the cast, just the lines that we cast, but not for fish just for that undying wish, for connection and trust, knowing and loving self is a must. Even as the time blows away, I have faith I am giving more positive energy today than I did yesterday. That the love I gave always helped to heal and save, love is still teaching me how to behave, kind and brave and honest to the grave. But man I got work to do, right now just gotta follow through. Need to be alone so more true colors are shown, love the way we have grown, but I am not yours to own, I choose freedom and the unknown.

Inspire Within, Inquire Within

Response Time

Say something if you please,
say something would you please?
Friendship is delicate,
it's all relative and relevant.
Making self better
through the act of being together,
two souls or more tethered
like birds of a feather,
but the feathers still shed,
some ends go dead,
some show a different head
when they get ahead.
Some hide when they get behind,
beaten by the tide
is when we need to be able to confide
but we hide. Instead let's take a ride,
no destination just to enjoy company,
my destiny is full of real people loving me.
I give my love so freely,
no really say something If you please,
say something, would you please?

Heartbreak I am Not Supposed to Have

Fell in and got broken before anything began,
Love as fast as I can, hurts so much I cant stand.
Became her biggest fan and then she ran.
Never should've happened due to the state,
Maybe we rushed or maybe we were too late.
Either way here I am with these pieces again,
Puzzling them together the best I can.
I have never been anything like most men,
Not afraid to be vulnerable when
New experiences just begin.
Make mistakes pretty often,
Growing as responsible as a human can.
Ultimately I am still an imperfect man.
You came in like a thief in the night,
Eagerly I shared my love and light.
You shared back and it felt more than right.
Never based in physicality,
we were attracted to the reality,
And the fantasy we could both see,
Well not so clearly apparently.
Both stuck in places we didn't want to be,
Thank you so much for helping me!
With my own decision and clarity.
I know my heart should not be broken,
But with the type of words that were spoken
And now that I keep myself this open.
It'd be a lie to say I was not hopin'...
It would lead somewhere.
Not gonna whine that life isn't fair,

Inspire Within, Inquire Within

I think you're just scared,
And I understand because I am too.
No matter what I'll care,
And I'm still grateful that I fell for you.
Heartbreak I'm not supposed to have
And trust I haven't explained the half.

New Normal

As the blue and green swirl
this boy met a girl,
Both wrapped in self deception,
yet gave birth to immaculate conception.
I'm still sorry I let you down,
just wanted to give her a crown,
and make this castle for my son...
For my son I am still not done,
never done until I've died, learned or won...
No illusions or confusion,
I worship women and sometimes too much,
let em use me as a crutch
while I use 'em for the same, pretty much.
We're all in a rush
to turn our heart and brain to mush.
Get wrapped up in a tiny crush
'cause they make us blush...
still wanna make you proud,
still wanna scream real loud,
but I'm stuck in this cloud.

In between, in between
kind and mean,
between saint and fiend,
tech support corporate drone,
just wanna make it past being unknown,
wanna get rid of this world I never condoned,
never acted like I was grown,
lost boy old soul sinner,
trying to give up my sleep and dinner,
to become a spiritual winner,
won't let this fire grow dimmer.

Summer Storm

Cloudy days should not phase,
even without the blinding rays,
look for the diverse ways this world can amaze,
Here lemme me rephrase...
when the grey starts dulling the green,
hiding the sun's bright sheen,
spirit is never fooled by that smoke screen,
Sunlight still finds our eyes
even when it is not seen.
Whatever paint splattered upon the sky's canvas,
Everyday is another way
to better understand this,
earth on her axis
with balanced mix of pain and Bliss,
so many lessons to catch or miss.
Awareness is the key,
to unlock all potential and ability,

Inspire Within, Inquire Within
always available to you and me,
the sacred technology
inside each moving sea
And growing tree,
trying to explain every way to get free,
metaphors to visualize easily like 1.2.3.
using A-Z just to find a way to be.
Never hide away or flee,
here to Enhance the world and the way I see.
Rainy days matter to me,
just like any other opportunity,
to find the beauty and unity.

Introverted Social Butterfly

Crowded rooms make me feel lonely,
I hate being perceived as phony,
I am the one and only. M-E an M.C.
and Authenticity is super important to me,
old ignorance is the only fee,
along the journey there will be growing pains,
takes sweat and blood to break any chains.
Takes a lot of momentum to derail these trains.
Remember we can shine even when it rains,
let's take back our hearts and brains,
let's navigate and plot the soul,
at least that's my main goal,
as the 'beautiful struggle' continues to unfold.
I am personally at the threshold,
of finding ways to project and remold,
I am forcefully uncontrolled,
no duality of reward or scold,
my light will never be sold!
Just like true love never gets old!

Let YourSelf

Creativity came to stay,
teaching the serious how to play,
teaching night how to dance with the day.
Teaching destruction new ways to slay,

sculpting selective chaos outta clay.
Talents and failures on full display,
both the sinner and the saint,
the pictures that we paint,
helped us figure how to make the record rotate,
words and music found their soul's mate,
they all relate as we create, so please create!
For the sake of your fate, let yourself create
whatever your deeper self tells you to make,
for no person should you be fake
or anything less than God's stake,
Lessons and gifts given for your sake.
Let yourself create.

Poetry Practice

Mastering Metaphor and simile
Exercised through autonomy,
Therapy powerfully distilling me.
Climbing lights ladder
balanced with dark matter,
mixing all the right ingredients into the batter,
baking miracles with verbs,
rolled up just like the best herbs,
breathing skylines and stretching spines,
moving forward as our universe aligns.

Inspire Within, Inquire Within

Educate to Elevate

Education needs to be free,
let's go to war with poverty,
stop being so worried about property,
shine a light on all the spiritual robbery.
Never conform, stay informed.
We gotta stay positive proactively,
not allowing society to give our children this mental radioactivity.
Can't cover eyes from all this Injustice,
let's face it all we really have is just us.
Communities dedicated to unity,
individuals trying to make love indivisible,
make the truth more visible.
Rebuild on principles that are more sensible.
Shared respect and trust,
cease the greed and blood lust.
It's up to us to use whatever gifts we possess,
to fear less and stop being fooled by those with excess.
Allowing our voices to be suppressed,
instead, let's connect and coalesce.
We are the foundation, we are a creative creation,
let's lead ourselves into a new calibration
with a love-centered adaptation!
I know I am more than a paycheck,
I know we are more than an unplanned wreck,
everything we are is evolving...
Intuitions energy is calling as the earth keeps revolving.

Hero's True Battle

Bound in chains of my own purpose,
'til all the fear and hate disperses.
Externalizing demons to slice 'em up,
sacrifice my heart to kill the corrupt,
no more storing fires gotta let it erupt.
Hero with no need for a mask,
answering questions my spirit has to ask.
Breaking down dreams into tasks,
in the truths rays my light body basks.
Rudraksha beads and crystal armor,
raising heads like a snake charmer.
If Motivation is a crop I am the farmer.
Accepting my karma and dharma,
tearing down fake government and big pharma...
Symbolic like lotus pose,
tearing down mental walls with my prose,
as the light glows, scent of the rose,
leading us through the throes,
accepting and aware of where the journey goes,
never will I close my heart and mind,
this change is up to us to find.
I put the past behind and put all my efforts toward the present grind,
the cold world makes it hard to stay kind,
discipline helps to keep in line,
habits helping to redefine.
Blades dripping from the lies I had to cut through,
can't miss the loved ones I outgrew,

Inspire Within, Inquire Within

can't be afraid to say things just 'cause society makes it taboo,
don't let anyone suppress your sharp point of view.
Make sure they see the legacy you drew
after you've done all that you can do.

Trusty Words

Trusty words trusty words,
even when people run away in herds,
words are reliable although self always has to remember it's liable,
for any slander or libel.
Greatness I am executing while I cease the persecuting.
The silence inspires while the second-hand spins its tires,
bouncing on dusty wires, sitting around pit fires.
Words carry emotions and desires,
words inspire imagery, words inspire energy,
might as well make the words positive,
fill the words with love!
Fill the words with smiles!
Even if you think you've walked the wrong miles,
can't turn back the dials, although words can help reconcile,
constructed pattern like tile, gonna let these words spin for a while.
One day maybe I'll meet a woman that can be as reliable as words,
until then I will just appreciate the birds,
as they fly past me, fly free,
just like the words that seem to escape me.

Common Sense

Common sense ain't been common for ages,
so distracted and perplexed it is outrageous.
We have to distribute,
positive feedback and tribute.
Your tribe is people that fit you,
so many to give honor to,
I honor you!

Opportunities

7 days in a week,
everyone is unique,
a million chances to speak,
always perfecting my technique.
There's an eternity to seek,
within each part,
of your soul and heart.
You failed? so what?! Restart!
Use the frustration to fuel your art,
up to us to outsmart,
problems before they tear us apart.

Inspire Within, Inquire Within

A.R.T.

A-R-T isn't hard to see,
constantly surrounding you and me,
bringing me serenity,
helping find my true identity.
Have to mention, the path to my Ascension,
is through pain loss and tension,
so I'm ready to be met with apprehension.
Building on comprehension
how to scratch the surface of the 4th dimension,
focused on awareness and attention.
Art is my only weapon,
against demons inside of me,
and any powers that be.
Trying to stop us from being free,
trying to control the beauty we see,
only I can define what beauty is to me.
A-R-T Can't spell earth or heart without the word art.
And every single day you wake up is a fresh start.
Only you can stop you from making your mark.

Questions

Has life left you feeling unfulfilled?
What is it that you are trying to build?
How did your creator make you skilled?
What makes your heart feel thrilled?

If you don't know, who should I ask?
Are you fixated on the past?
Can I see you or are you wearing a mask?
How long do you think the charade will last?
Do you practice self expression?
How do you fight your depression?
Can't be afraid to question,
"What direction do I need the most progression?"
How do you deal with anger and aggression?
Does it take you forever to learn a lesson?
Are you aware of every blessing?
Or too focused on the stressing?
Do you believe in dragons angels and elves?
Do you believe in yourselves?
What section would you be in life's bookshelves?
I think mine is a comedy,
where we laugh at all the hypocrisy,
true characters making no apology,
just being who we gotta be!
What will be our collective legacy? Destiny?
How 'bout You be the best you and I'll be the best me.
Let us set our potential free!

Commitment

Commitment is a depth of conviction,
can create inspiration for those with vision.
Depending on how you're living.
Truth is stranger than fiction,
just don't be a contradiction.

Inspire Within, Inquire Within

If you say you're going to be or do,
then actually follow through,
it's okay to let people down sometimes,
we're all perfectly imperfect,
it's how we atone for our crimes,
be forgiving when you're giving the verdict.
Commitment attains dreams,
but make sure you're committed to the right things,
not just doing it 'cause the way it seems,
growth is what every miracle brings.
Settle for nothing less,
you were born blessed and deserve the best.

Brighter Dawn

Inspiration rainin' like cats and dogs,
I am using these words as Lincoln logs,
building with every bit I get,
giving it living it
'cause I'm never gon' be a hypocrite.
Givin' every ounce of self
that God will permit,
getting rid of the pieces that never fit,
getting so much support but you can't see it,
like I'm on stage and they're chilling in the orchestra pit.
Calibrated on our mission to uplift,
not allowing focus to drift!
Propelling change, with no need for receipt,
fair exchange, in a world more complete.

Living to the rhythm of our hearts beat,
not limited by what's in our bank or on our timesheet,
making commitments that are concrete.
Giving everyone a seat, at the round table,
where we work together to make this planet stable,
little things that we are more than able,
to do, to get through, it's up to me and you!
To be the phenomenon that chooses to act on
the schematics that need to be redrawn
until we reach a brighter dawn.

Quality

Let's bring some quality and honesty **back** to our policies,
Education and safety need to be free commodities!
No more hiding behind a veil like an electoral college,
ultimately we need the truth to be common knowledge.
We need to shed light on all the atrocity
happening in and outside the borders of our country.
Replace this mindset of Monopoly
into a Culture of reciprocity.
Banish this evil and allow our innocence to flourish
into innovators we encourage and nourish!
We love getting addicted
so let's get addicted to the truth!
A healthy habit we can hand down to the youth.
Start constantly seeing consciously,
facing the world more honestly,
as we get better at communicating
and leading the youth using that same truth.

Inspire Within, Inquire Within

Open Door

Door is unlocked no need to knock,
got warmth and love in stock,
to combat trauma and Aftershock.
Activist poet like 2pac,
here to shake the bedrock,
of every single block,
programmed with negative self talk.
Taught to always quit or stop,
doing things that make you feel on top,
our art is delicate like a raindrop.
Hoping to land in some fresh crop
and not get stuck on a rooftop,
but even then; perspective can help you again,
see the brighter side, of this uncontrollable ride.
Every view can be modified, together we can turn any tide.
Those still asleep will be mystified,
evolution at the pace of a landslide with nowhere to hide.
Together we can turn the tide but we have to be more unified.

Milk and Honey

The present need is so prevalent,
for a human race more benevolent,
not acting like other struggles are irrelevant.
This land of milk and honey has gone sour
and I hate the smell of it.

But most still buying and selling it,
decisive too! Never just for the hell of it.
Rather than get stuck
in conspiracy theories,
let's try to see clearly
and write a better series,
power in word but no need to fear these,
just hear me out here please.
Up to all of us to choose,
the direction we shall cruise,
whether we fulfill or we fail,
together we all sail.
Magnetized to this loving globe,
flying around on this galactic road,
or should I say being towed,
like the other satellites,
by our big love light.
We should try to mirror the sun's flight,
progression every single day and night,
fearlessly guiding us into the unknown,
unhappy with fate then make your own!
Want to go fast go alone,
wanna go far go together,
so let's change the weather, together,
let's stop just doing whatever, together. Together!
The present need is so prevalent,
for a human race more benevolent.
This land of milk and honey has gone sour
And I hate the smell of it.

Silver Lining

Transparent with open eyes,
in a time cloudy with lies,
sent here to help harmonize,
for my mistakes I apologize,
but necessary to make it to this state of mind.
They say that this state of mine,
is for lovers!
but most must be hiding under covers,
'cause the ignorance is easier to discover.
Helps to see the silver lining,
when life's track is on the wrong timing,
never resigning I am realigning,
the creative control of what I am designing.

Last Words

If you only had a few minutes or maybe seconds left,
to spit out one last thought with your very last breath.
What would you say, would it be pertinent to today?
Are you willing to let those words stay,
part of your legacy forever,
or would it just be a strong goodbye
to help the ties sever.
would it be full of love or regret?
what would you want to remember or forget?
Where are heart and mind set?

How many soul mates have you met?
How are you going to let?
The river of life tell your tale,
was it all rocky seas or did you enjoy a smooth sail?
How would you grade yourself if we pass or fail?
In the afterlife do we get to send spirit mail?
If you only have one mark you make,
is it an opportunity that you will take?
Can't be afraid to shake,
the idea of what's real and fake,
and question everything for your own sake.
Get as close as you can to feeling like nothing was a mistake.

Write Like You Live, Live Your message!

Writing any and every where I can,
writing endlessly until I break through this hand,
writing forward to the future better man,
who will see these words and inner stand.
Writing until the words blur and overlap,
gushing out of me sticky like tree sap.
Words that I adore
and words that can pierce the core,
words that can destroy
and words meant simply to enjoy.
Writing was no longer enough so I began reciting,
every time performing is so exciting,
found The Venue 35 tribe who were instantly inviting,
diverse expressions for the struggle we're all fighting!

Inspire Within, Inquire Within

Each interaction linked to a chained reaction,
joining a community ready for positive action,
only furthering my attraction.
To every part of this process
to remind self that I am blessed
and have overflowing love to give,
a message I have to not only share but live!

Live the Life

Life ain't a party until you participate,
how you relate is based on how you create,
please meditate on what makes you great.
I am a thought that became alive,
I am an engine that will drive,
further away from a mentality to only survive,
learn to learn grow and/or thrive.
Show me the deep end and I dive,
spitting bars that burn the hate,
manifesting change before it's too late.
Find someone to elevate,
give people purpose when you delegate,
together we can better investigate
and innovate the current state!
Of affairs, Aura shooting soul flares,
finding folks that share my cares.
We found a way to spin new dreams from old nightmares,
love and trust, nothing compares.

Message Isn't Written or Performed, it is Lived

Whether a pen or mic in my hand,
let fire free flow through,
hearts only demand,
is that I give truth to you.
Perception dictates direction,
we are the universe's introspection, taking a nice hard look in while
throwing us genetic evolution.
Yet some people obsessed with ignorance's pollution,
don't be part of the problem. Be the solution,
humanity's retribution. With no need for a violent revolution,
DNA releasing cerebral changes,
as the collective soul rearranges,
giving our lady the breath of fresh air she needs.
Let us respect our elders and new seeds,
person is more than their appearance and deeds.

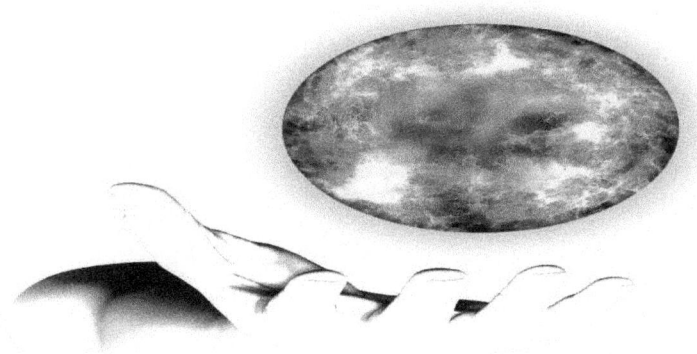

Inspire Within, Inquire Within

Inspire Within, Inquire Within

<u>Why Do You Try So Hard?</u>

Free spirits always going to reach,
Universe inside of each,
live, love, learn and teach.
Unbuilt all the unneeded fear and guilt,
patching together a better quilt,
soft and strong,
admitting when I am wrong.
Celebrate success of self and others,
recognize my struggle in another's,
appreciate both my sister and brothers,
unique views, always trying to decipher the clues,
their love language and life from their shoes.
Get better at picking up the cues,
when God gives me good news.
I want to be the voice and hand,
that helps people from every land,
filling my souls demand,
by working harder than I think I can.
Broadening the concepts I understand,
by combining awareness with action,
no more distraction
or need for immediate satisfaction,
I want to be the spark of a new chain reaction.

Fault Lines

Our fault lines are what make us Divine,
through the cracks is how we share our shine,
so happy the sun's combines with mine.
Sun Combines with yours,
as our universe explores.
Even as the rain pours,
even when you hide indoors.
Through the cracks is how we share our shine,
our fault lines are what make us Divine.

Apologies

Never thought I'd be a heartbreaker,
wasn't meant to deal with any faker,
anyone not willing to give, always a taker.
I've always been a mover and shaker,
a creator thanks to the creator.
No time to wait til later,
give love to the lover and the hater,
haters need fulfillment like bulbs need a filament.
Use the Divine instrument, find the right sentiment,
and start to implement every authentic intent.
Every self element is relevant,
love yourself through heaven and the hell-of-it.

Reminders

Poems and emotions remind me of strength in fragility.
Gratitude and giving remind me of heavenly ability.
Pain in my chest reminds me of my mortality.
Got a lot left to do in this version of reality.

Perfect Union

Sun making love to the earth,
she lets the light in for all it's worth.
Hard work to give perpetual rebirth,
paired with shared mirth.
Dancing around the milky way,
won't allow their shared stare to slip away.
Always immersed in what we call today,
with their apparent passion on display.

Hip Hop Day Dream

Circled around the same street twice,
almost stumbled on two blind mice,
both trying to find a slice,
both willing to sacrifice,
admit didn't listen to any of their advice.
My new thoughts had their feet in ice.

Spitting science through visualizations,
spiritual artistic interpretations,
I hesitate to call em realizations,
we'll say dream actualizations
for all nations relations and perceptual stations.
Taking the beat and giving birth to new creations.

<u>Forbidden</u>

What feels forbidden is dying to be written,
that thing you're most afraid to write,
is what you should put down before the end of the night,
whether it feels wrong or right, truth belongs in the light.
Whether it's expressing both sides of an internal fight,
put it on paper so you can get more objective sight!
Remind yourself everything is gonna be alright,
this is all just for you to gain insight,
others will only know if you invite.
Them to read or you choose to recite,
those words you are most afraid to write.

Inspire Within, Inquire Within

Earth day

She was just a simple stone,
floating on her own.
Always really admired
the way she found the sun's fire.
Or maybe the sun found her,
while the perfect system started to stir.
The moon not knowing what's in store,
understandably attracted to her perfect core.
We're protected by her auras energy dome,
Utopian home for all creatures that swim fly or roam.
Need Food? our lady grows her own, love is freely shown,
abundance of air and water freely given,
continue to be polluted by the way we're livin'.
She has planted some seeds that are holistically driven,
to unlock the powers that have always been hidden.
Inside of ourselves and inside of our planet,
so trust in spirit and don't ever panic.
Plenty of challenges and blessings we've been handed,
and we are never truly stranded,
but for real change we all have to demand it.

Easter

Day devoted to Resurrection,
some use it for greed's collection,
others choose light rejection,
please see the beauty in the reflection,

we can learn alot from introspection,
we can go far when we choose a direction,
not about perfection...
Start with one small section
of the bigger picture,
seeing between the lines of each scripture,
focused on the holy ghost fixture,
hanging somewhere between my soul and heart,
inspiring me to turn my life into art,
helping everyone enjoy their part,
In this grand play, we call earth for today.
Ceaselessly I pray,
everything turns out the very best way!

Picturing the Spirit

If you ask me spirits look like nebulas in anthropomorphic form,
like a beautifully controlled lightning storm.
Helping to keep our eyes open and hearts warm,
in whatever purpose we're sent to perform,
giving us more power than an entire swarm.
We are each unique, never meant to conform!
No weapon shall be formed!
"Energy never ceases to exist,
it only changes forms." - A. Einstein once explained,
soul can only be temporarily contained,
an idea that became ingrained,
into my perception of reality,
before we picked from the knowledge tree,

to whatever is beyond infinity.
Just a silly samurai trying to figure out the how and why,
how to fly, INFJ an advocate dragon gemini,
that's Meyers Briggs if you need to verify,
more effects than a butterfly.
Unconditional love I exemplify,
mission is to identify
the steps it'll take to unify,
practicing my magic with intention to clarify,
simplify and open every sleeping eye
as we reach high, higher than the sky!
Passing the torch before we die,
never saying goodbye,
reincarnate again and continue to try.
"Energy never ceases to exist,
it only changes forms."

Life is a Dream

Life! It is all a dream!
too many projectors hogging the screen,
not acting as a team,
so we're stuck swimming upstream,
until we balance every beam,
and manifest a healing scene,
empower youth with self esteem!
IT IS ALL A DREAM,
change is more possible than it would seem.

Shadow and Shine

We make the spiritual so complicated
when in reality if scientifically educated.
You already realize,
while material can mesmerize,
there's still no proof it exists at all,
it's just a tale that's tall,
yet every day we answer the call,
of every impulse we're victim to insults,
not saying the world is false,
just saying there's more
than chemicals and electrical signals.
Don't wait for something to align,
create your own design,
start from the deepest inside,
redefine and refine.
Don't wait for a sign
to balance your shadow and shine,
this world is mine
and all of yours
hiding in your cores,
so why are we crawling on all fours
when we could be flying like in folklore.

Inspire Within, Inquire Within

Colophon
Brought to you by Wider Perspectives Publishing, care of James Wilson, with the mission of advancing the poetry and creative community of Hampton Roads, Virginia.
See our production of works from …

Tanya Cunningham
    (Scientific Eve)
Terra Leigh
Ray Simmons
Samantha Borders-Shoemaker
Taz Waysweete'
Bobby K. (The Poor Man's Poet)
J. Scott Wilson (TEECH!)
Zach Crowe
Charles Wilson
Jorge Mendez & JT Williams
Sarah Eileen Williams
Stephanie Diana (Noftz)
the Hampton Roads
    Artistic Collective
Jason Brown (Drk Mtr)
Martina Champion
Tony Broadway
Ken Sutton
Crickyt J. Expression
Gloria Darlene Mann
Samantha Giovjian Clarke
Cassandra IsFree
Neil Spirtas
Lisa M. Kendrick

… and others to come soon.

We promote and support poetic artists
from the seats, from the stands,
from the snapping fingers and clapping hands
from the pages, and the stages
and now we pass them forth to the ages

Stop it James, Just stop it

Check for the above artists on FaceBook, the Virginia Poetry Online channel on YouTube, and other social media.

Hampton Roads Artistic Collective is the non-profit extension of WPP and strives to simultaneously support worthy causes and the creative artists.

www.ingramcontent.com/pod-product-compliance
Lightning Source LLC
Chambersburg PA
CBHW031422160426
43196CB00008B/1017